Contents

Going to waste

Natural resources such as wood, metals, oil and gas are used to make all kinds of things we use every day. We often throw these things away without a thought, creating waste that ends up in a variety of different places.

We all produce a vast amount of rubbish every year. Landfill sites like the one above will rapidly fill up unless we start reducing the amount we throw away.

Where does it go?

Litter

Some waste is thrown carelessly and lies around as litter. Litter looks bad, it blocks up drains and can be dangerous to animals and people.

Landfill

Large amounts of rubbish are taken to holes in the ground called landfill sites.

Rubbish can take years to rot. As waste rots, poison leaks into the soil and poisonous gases escape into the air. These gases affect our climate by causing global warming. Landfill sites are also expensive to control and maintain.

Incinerators

Incinerators are big fires or furnaces where rubbish is burnt, sending smoke into the air and creating ash that has to be got rid of.

The Green Team

Reduce, Reuse

Sally Hewitt

FRANKLIN WATTS
LONDON • SYDNEY

First published in 2008 by
Franklin Watts
338 Euston Road
London NW1 3BH

Franklin Watts Australia
Level 17/207 Kent Street
Sydney NSW 2000

Editor: Jeremy Smith
Design: Jason Anscomb

A CIP catalogue record for this book
is available from the British Library.

Picture credits: Alamy: 6, 7b, 8, 10 all, 11 all, 18 all, 19, 21tr, 22 all,
23 all, 24. Corbis: 14. Computers for Schools: 17b. Freecycle: 9b & t. Friends of Malawi
Orphans: 15 all. istockphoto: 21tl. Shutterstock: OFC, 3, 7t, 9r, 12, 16, 17t. St Joseph's
School: 13 all. Trafalgar Infant & Junior School: 26-27 all. Wonga Beach School: 20 all.

Dewey Classification: 941.085

ISBN: 978 0 7496 7937 8

Printed in China

Franklin Watts is a division of Hachette Children's Books,
an Hachette Livre UK company
www.hachettelivre.co.uk.

Not all this rubbish needs to go into landfill. Some of it could easily be recycled or reused.

Action!

Make a rubbish diary.

Record what goes into the bin at home and in your classroom under these headings:

- Glass
- Paper and card
- Plastic
- Food and garden waste
- Textiles
- Other.

Don't drop litter. Take it home with you or put it in the bin or recycling point.

Too much rubbish

Households, shops and factories all produce rubbish. Some rubbish, such as food and paper, is biodegradable. This means it breaks down naturally over time and disappears. Other rubbish, made of materials such as glass, metal and plastic, is non-biodegradable, which means it stays around for hundreds of years.

Challenge!

You can help.

- Reduce means to make less.
- Reduce the rubbish you throw away at home.
- Reduce the rubbish your class throws away at school.

Make less rubbish

To join the green team, one of the most useful things you can do is to reduce, or make less, rubbish in the first place. You can start at the shops.

Challenge!

Think before you buy something new.

Ask yourself:

- Do I really need it?
- Have I already got one?
- Can I borrow one?
- How many times will I use it?
- Can I use something else instead?
- How long will I be interested in it?

When you've answered all those questions, ask yourself, do I still want to buy it?

Throw away

People say we live in a 'throw-away society'. This means we use things and then throw them away, sometimes when they are still quite new. But you can change that. First of all, try not to buy so much!

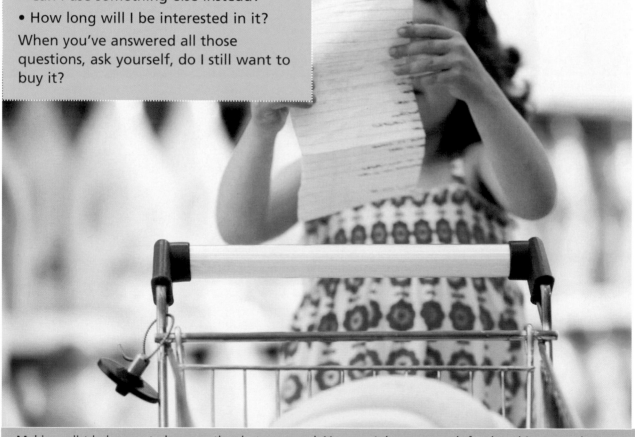

Making a list helps you to buy exactly what you need. You won't buy too much food or things you don't need that you will throw away without even using.

Don't throw out usable things you don't want any more.

- Hold a sale and give the money you make to an environmental charity.
- Join an organisation such as Freecycle and give usable things away.

Freecycle

Cut down on what you throw away. The Freecycle Network was founded in May 2003 in Tuscan, USA, to help save desert landscape from being taken over by landfill sites. Today, there are Freecycle groups all over the world. They try to keep usable things out of landfill sites by passing them on to someone who will use them. Their aim is to reduce the number of things we make and buy.

At this Freecycle event, everyone brought along stuff they didn't want and other people took it home and reused it.

Pete   Jack

Jack's feet will grow and his roller blades will soon be too small for him. He can borrow a pair from his older brother Pete, and pass his onto someone else when they are too small for him. That way, he will make less rubbish than if he buys a new pair.

Packaging and wrapping

Most of the rubbish we throw away is packaging. Reducing the amount of packaging we bring into our homes and schools will help to reduce the waste mountain.

Food is one of the most packaged things we buy. Packaging makes the food more expensive, and leads to more litter (above right).

Food packaging

Food packaging helps to preserve, protect and keep food fresh. But a lot of the packaging is not necessary and can create litter that does not rot away.

Learn to cook

Ready-cooked meals come in lots of packaging. Cooking from fresh ingredients saves packaging and is usually a healthier choice.

School supplies

School supplies arrive in all kinds of packaging. Cardboard and paper are biodegradable and recyclable, but polystyrene balls and bubble wrap are not.

Learn how to cook using fresh ingredients. Not only does this create less waste but the food tastes better, too!

Magazines

Magazines and comics can be read again and again. Don't throw yours away. Find out if your doctor's surgery, hospital or any other waiting room wants them and pass them on. Don't buy the same magazines or comics as your friends. Each buy a different one and share.

Case study – Read To Grow and Book Aid

If you don't want your books, there is always someone else who does. There are many schools all over the world who have very few books and urgently need more.

Read To Grow and Book Aid are charities that send books to schools in developing countries. St Joseph's Primary School in Glasgow, Scotland, is part of the Read to Grow scheme. In 2004, they won the World Book Day Award for collecting the highest number of books in any school.

➤ Action!

Get your school to collect good quality used books.

• Choose a charity that will help you to send them to a school abroad.

• Use the Internet and email to make friends with children at the school.

• Maybe they will be able to help your school in return?

Children from St Joseph's celebrate their award.

A school chart shows how many books have been collected.

Some of the books collected by St Joseph's ended up at Tokokoe Library in Ghana, Africa. Here are the children showing off some of their new books.

Clothes and shoes

Children often grow out of their clothes and shoes while they are still almost new. Don't throw away clothes and shoes that are still in good condition but are too small for you. There will always be a child somewhere who will be able to make good use of them.

Challenge!

Sort through your clothes.

• Too small? Take them to a charity shop, give them to a friend or your younger brother or sister.

• Torn? Put them in a pile for mending.

• Stained? Put them in the recycling bin.

Mend, alter and decorate

Before you throw out your old clothes and shoes, see if you can you mend, alter or decorate them and give them a new life. It can be fun. Add a bright, interesting patch to a tear or a hole. Embroider a flower, add ribbons or pin on badges. Send worn shoes to the mender or buy new laces.

Mend clothes rather than throwing them out and buying new ones.

School uniforms

Does your school have a uniform? If so, yours could be used again and again. Make sure as many children as possible wear your uniform after you have grown out of it. Charities including Oxfam now run uniform recycling schemes that help people in poorer countries afford an education.

Eilidh Whiteford, Oxfam in Scotland's Campaign Manager, says: "Money raised by the sales of recycled school uniforms can help ensure more children receive the right of a free education."

Case study – Friends of Malawi Orphans (FOMO)

A charity called Friends of Malawi Orphans helps children in Malawi, Africa, by providing them with recycled clothes from all over the United Kingdom. FOMO also has its own sewing school in Malawi, where the children are taught to make some parts of their school clothes themselves, teaching them valuable skills for the future.

Action!

Set up a uniform exchange or sale at school.

• If you hold a sale you can send the money to buy uniforms so children can go to school in another part of the world.

FOMO at work

Clothes are collected and packaged up ready to send to Malawi.

Children are taught how to repair and alter clothes, a valuable skill.

Whole schools are given matching uniforms.

Paper

Paper is made from wood. It helps the environment to use paper made of wood from forests that can be replanted or to use recycled paper. But it's even better to use less paper!

The pine trees growing in this plantation have been planted as a crop. They are cut down to be made into paper and new young trees are replanted in their place.

Ancient woodlands

Ancient woodlands are home to a great variety of plants and animals such as these dormice. If trees are cut down to make paper, the animals lose their home. Even if new trees are planted, these create a different kind of habitat and many of the plants and animals never return.

Challenge!

Use less paper.
• Think before you print.
• If you do print, use both sides of the paper.
• Write notes on a chalk board or wipe-clean board.
• Save wrapping paper and use it again.
• Never throw paper away – reuse or recycle it.

Stop junk mail.
• Find out how your home can register to stop receiving junk mail (unwanted post that is trying to sell something).
• You could put a note on your door or window that says – **NO JUNK MAIL!**

Wood is transported around the world. This process uses a lot of energy.

Make homemade paper.

This is a good way of reusing paper.

You will need:

- Used paper
- A bowl of warm water
- An egg beater or liquidiser
- A rectangle of fine mesh
- 2 large sheets of blotting paper
- An iron

• Tear the used paper into small pieces.

• Soak the pieces in a bowl of warm water for about 10 minutes.

• Beat the mixture with an egg beater or liquidise it to make pulp.

• Lower the mesh into the bowl then lift out. It should be covered in an even layer of pulp.

• Leave the mesh to drain.

• Turn the layer of pulp onto a sheet of blotting paper.

• Cover it with the other sheet of blotting paper, then iron with a warm iron.

• Lift off the top sheet of blotting paper then leave the pulp to dry for 24 hours. Now use the paper you have made.

Using energy

Wood is often imported, which means it is brought in from another country. Transporting the wood and then making it into paper uses up fuel and causes pollution. Making new paper from old paper uses much less energy.

Waste paper

Paper and card rot in landfill sites and produces methane, a greenhouse gas that goes into the air and contributes to global warming. Reusing paper helps avoid this.

 **Action!**

Pupils and teachers can work together to reduce and reuse paper.

Ask your school to only buy recycled paper or paper from renewable forests.

Make a list of all the ways you could reduce your school's use of these paper goods:

– Exercise books

– Toilet paper

– Paper for art and craft.

Now put your list into action!

Plastic bags

About 1 trillion plastic bags are used around the world every year. Many bags end up as litter blowing in the wind and floating in the sea and rivers. Plastic from plastic bags stays in the environment for at least 100 years.

Members of Wonga Beach State School in Queensland, Australia reduced the number of plastic bags they used and the amount of waste in general.

Case study – Wonga Beach State School

Wonga Beach State School in far north Queensland, Australia won a prize for cutting down on the amount of plastic bags used in 2007. "Enviro Dollars" were given out to students for reducing waste and for bringing litter-free lunches to school. Recyclable items were also cleaned out and put in the recycling bin. Community businesses donated new items and at the end of the school year the students were able to buy the items with their Enviro Dollars.

Challenge!

Do a plastic bag survey at home.

• How many plastic bags have you got at home?

• How many do you bring home each week?

• How many do you throw away?

• How many do you reuse?

• Can you reduce the number of new plastic bags you use?

A set of Enviro Dollars used by pupils at the Wonga Beach State School.

Oil

Oil is used to make the plastic used for bags. Reducing and reusing plastic bags will help to save oil, a precious natural resource.

Plastic bags can choke and suffocate people as well as wildlife. Keep them away from young children. Make sure any you use are punctured with small holes to let in air.

Two swans fight over a plastic bag, mistaking it for food.

We depend on oil for fuel and to make plastic, but there is only a limited amount left.

Helping the environment

Reducing the number of plastic bags we use will help to keep the environment free of poisonous and dangerous litter. Plastic is a man-made material. It won't biodegrade like natural materials. Plastic bags break down into small, poisonous pieces that end up in the soil, the sea, rivers, sand and shingle where birds and fish accidentally eat them. Plastic bags floating in the sea look like jellyfish which are food to many sea animals. The animals eat the plastic bags and are poisoned, or choke on them.

Action!

Use your old plastic bags to make one big, very strong bag.

• Ask an adult to help you cut plastic bags into strips. Use the strips to knit, crochet, weave or plait a new strong bag.

• Have a competition at school for the best reused plastic bag design.

• Buy a couple of textile shopping bags and remember to use them instead of asking for a plastic shopping bag.

Toys

Toys help you to use your imagination and learn new things.
You can play with them by yourself or with friends. It is much better for the environment make your own toys or reuse old ones. Making new toys and games uses up lots of energy and natural resources.

An old bicycle wheel makes a good hoop to bowl along.

Make your own games

Some of the best games need only your imagination. Others can be made from objects lying around the home, with no need to buy anything new. It is easy to make an Oware set like the one opposite. Use two egg boxes (for 6 eggs) to make a board of two rows of "cells". Then find 48 seeds or beans and put four in each cell. The object of the game is to capture more seeds than your opponent. To find out the rules of the game go to www. wikipedia.org/oware.

This is a traditional Oware board and pieces. Make your own from objects around the house.

Are you playing with the toys you've already got?

• Have a clear-out of your toy box.

• Find a new home for toys that you only sometimes or never play with. Take them to a charity shop or to your school sale.

• You can give toys in good condition to a toy library.

Case study – A toy library

Rather than put your toys in a cupboard when you get bored with them, why not let someone else enjoy them? Lots of charities collect toys and games. UNRWA (the United Nations Relief and Works Agency for Palestine Refugees in the Near East) is setting up 11 toy libraries in the war-torn Gaza Strip in Israel to provide places where around 3,800 children will be able to enjoy playing safely. The centres will also create new opportunities for women, children and the disabled to join in with their local communities having fun together.

An UNRWA toy library full of second-hand toys ready for children to enjoy.

Batteries

Toys often need batteries to make them work. Batteries are packs of chemicals. When batteries are thrown away the chemicals can leak into the soil. Find out where batteries can be disposed of responsibly. Buy rechargeable batteries that can be reused again and again. Use solar-powered batteries, which are re-charged by sunlight.

Most electric toys use batteries. Opt for rechargeable rather than disposable ones.

Challenge!

Use your imagination.

Some toys can be played with again and again in all kinds of different ways. Try out these toys and games and discover that toys don't have to be expensive to be fun.

• Cards

• Oware/Mancala

• Skipping rope

• Football

• Kite

• Dressing-up box

• Marbles.

A green fair

You could organise your own green summer fair with a recycling theme. Invite the local community to share what you have learnt about what we can all do to save the planet.

Green team

One Junior School Green Team had lots of ideas for their stall. First they held a competition for the best object made from reused materials to be sold at the fair with prizes from a charity shop. They sold paper weights made from stones, driftwood signs, plants and flowers grown by the gardening club and shoe bags and aprons made from reused material.

Amber (4M):

"It was a good idea to get people to reuse their stuff to make stuff."

Emily (4M):

"Re-userific! I liked ... seeing all the things people had made from re-usable things. I loved the dream-catcher made from an old piece of wool, corks and see-through plastic paper."

Trafalgar Infant and Junior School's Green Summer Fair got everyone thinking about reducing, reusing and recycling.

Andy

Paul

Challenge!

Think up a competition that will encourage everyone at school to reduce and reuse.

How will you judge the winning entry?

Will it be:

- the most original and imaginative idea?
- the idea that makes best use of reusing things?
- the idea that everyone learns the most from?

How can the prize encourage the winner to carry on reducing and reusing?

The House of the Future designs were displayed at the fair so other people could share what the children had learnt.

Displays, posters and leaflets helped visitors to the Recycle stall learn about how recycling helps protect the environment.

House of the Future Competition

A competition to design a house of the future got the children thinking about eco-friendly materials and waste and energy saving ideas. Some homes already have solar panels to heat water, and wind turbines to make electricity.

Food

The food and drink stalls were planned to create as little rubbish as possible. Lunches were sold in brown paper bags that were recycled on the spot. Drinks were served in strong plastic cups that could be washed and reused.

Organisations

Organisations concerned with green issues will usually work with schools to help them learn about saving the planet and taking action. At this green fair, the local council, Friends of the Earth, Fairtrade and the local Environment Network joined together to set up stalls so people could find out about the work they do and get involved.

Action!

Plan a green fair for your school.

• How will you encourage people to reduce waste and reuse things?

• What stalls will there be?

• What events will you have?

• What food will you serve and how will you serve it?

• Who will you invite?

• What do you hope everyone will learn?

• How do you hope people will change what they do?

27

Glossary

Biodegrade
When something biodegrades, it breaks down naturally and becomes part of the soil, water or air. Vegetable peelings biodegrade but most plastic does not.

Developing country
A developing country is one that is mostly poor but is developing its schools, hospitals, farming and industry.

Exchange
When you exchange things, you give something and get something back in return. At a uniform exchange, you give the uniform you have grown out of and exchange it for one that fits you.

Greenhouse gas
Gases such as carbon dioxide that contribute to global warming.

Global warming
A rise in the Earth's temperature caused mainly by burning oil, gas and coal.

Habitat
A place where an animal or plant lives.

Landfill
A way of getting rid of waste by burying it in the ground.

Natural resource
Something that is useful to people found in nature such as oil and wood.

Polluting
Something is polluting if it harms the natural environment such as air, soil or water. Exhaust fumes from cars pollute the air. Oil spills at sea pollute the water.

Raw material
A natural material that things are made from, such as cotton, oil and wood.

Recharge
To refill with energy. Rechargeable batteries can be refilled with energy when they run out and used again.

Reduce
Reduce means to make less. Reducing the waste we make helps to reduce the amount of rubbish going into landfill.

Reuse
Reuse means to use again. If we reuse plastic bags, for example, it reduces the number being made and sent to landfill.

Weblinks

www.freecycle.org

More than 4,000 groups of freecyclers across the globe give and get stuff for free, reusing and keeping good things out of landfill sites. Find a group to join near where you live.

www.bookaid.org

Find out how you can donate books and help to give children all over the world the chance to read and learn.

www.oxfam.org.uk/coolplanet/kidsweb/oxfam/action.htm

Take your clothes, toys and other reusable stuff to an Oxfam shop near you. Money raised will help people all over the world.

www.fomo.co.uk

Friends of Mulanje Orphans collect clothes and school uniforms to help children in Malawi go to school.

www.eco-shools.org.uk

Your school can become part of an international group of schools committed to caring for the environment.

www.computeraid.org

Instead of throwing usable computers away, find out how they can be reused by schools and businesses in Africa.

www.olliesworld.com

A website for children to learn to reduce, reuse and recycle.

Note to parents and teachers:

Every effort has been made by the Publishers to ensure that these websites are suitable for children, that they are of the highest educational value, and that they contain no inappropriate or offensive material. However, because of the nature of the Internet, it is impossible to guarantee that the contents of these sites will not be altered. We strongly advise that Internet access is supervised by a responsible adult.

Index